THE
BIG
BOOK
OF THE
BLUE

Words and pictures
YUVAL ZOMMER

Sea life expert
BARBARA TAYLOR

Can you find ...

... exactly the same sardine
15 times in this book?
Watch out for imposters.

THE
BIG
BOOK
OF THE
BLUE

Thames & Hudson

WHO'S INSIDE?

OCEAN FAMILIES

What kinds of animals live in the ocean?

There are lots of animal families that live in the sea.

Some are hairy, some have scales, some have fins and some are boneless and brainless!

Mollusks ...

... include octupuses, squid, sea snails, oysters, clams and mussels

... have gills

... are cold blooded

... some live inside a shell

Crustaceans ...

... include crabs, lobsters, shrimp and krill

... have gills

... are cold blooded

... have a hard skeleton on the outside of their body

Fish ...

... include sharks, rays, swordfish, flying fish, seahorses, and pufferfish

... have gills

... are cold blooded

... have a skeleton of bone or cartilage

Mammals ...

... include seals,
whales and dolphins

... have lungs

... have furry or bristly skin

... are warm blooded

... have a bony skeleton

Reptiles ...

... include sea turtles and sea snakes

... have lungs

... are cold blooded

... have bones and scaly skin

FINS AND FLIPPERS

How do sea creatures move around?

Sea creatures move in all sorts of ways. Some use flippers, and fins, some use jet power and others simply float along. There are fast ones and slow ones and this all depends on the shape of their body and their swimming technique.

Fin-tastic

A fish bends its body to push itself along. It has fins for steering. A seahorse has tiny fins and swims slowly. It is the only fish that swims sitting upright.

Sss-wimming around

Eels and sea snakes wiggle their body in an s-shape to push against the water.

Flipping awesome

Dolphins, seals, whales and turtles all swim using flippers. Flippers have a wide flat surface, perfect for pushing against the water.

Bobbing along

A jellyfish pumps water in and out of its bell and bobs through the water.

Jet power

An octopus sucks water into its body and shoots it back out in a jet. This pushes it forward very quickly and its arms trail behind.

9

GILLS AND BLOWHOLES

How does an animal breathe underwater?

All animals need to breathe in oxygen to stay alive. Land animals get oxygen from the air. Some sea creatures come up to the surface to breathe in air but others filter oxygen out of the water.

Where there's a gill there's a way

Fish, squid and crabs breathe through gills. Gills are feathery flaps in an animal's body that take in water and filter out useful oxygen.

Breathable skin

Jellyfish, corals and sea anemones take in oxygen through their skin.

Coming up for air

Sea turtles, penguins and whales have lungs just like humans. This means that they need to come up to the surface to fill up their lungs with new air.

Blowholes

When a whale or dolphin comes up to breathe, it breathes out old, stale air. It does this through a blowhole on the top of its head.

Breath-holding champions

Some ocean animals come up for air every few minutes. A sperm whale can hold its breath for 2 hours!

SEA TURTLES

When is a turtle a sea turtle?

When it lives in the sea! A sea turtle has a smooth shell so it can move through water easily. It also can't hide its head inside its shell like other turtles.

Swim goggles

A sea turtle has see-through eyelids that it uses like a pair of goggles to see underwater!

GLIDING THROUGH WARM TROPICAL WATERS

Bouncing eggs

A sea turtle swims to shore to lay her eggs on the beach. They are made of a soft, bouncy material so that they don't break when they hit the sand.

Cutting edge

Turtles don't have teeth. Instead their jaws have razor-sharp edges that they use to slice through their food.

Did you know ...

... sea turtles can eat jellyfish without getting stung?

FLYING FISH

Does a flying fish really fly?

Yes! A flying fish flings itself out of the water to avoid being eaten by other fish. It glides through the air and flaps its fins. It can fly for up to 45 seconds.

Trick of the eye

A flying fish is blue on top so a bird flying above can't spot it against the sea. It has a silver tummy so it looks like the sky to a hungry fish swimming below.

Aerial attack!

A flying fish is never safe from predators. Even when it is flying, a bird might try and catch it.

Speedy torpedo

To launch its streamlined body into the sky, a flying fish has to be swimming at 37 miles per hour!

One big family

A flying fish swims in a school of up to one million others.

15

SEAHORSES

Is a seahorse a horse?

No! A seahorse is an upright type of fish.
It has a head like a horse, a grippy tail like
a monkey and a pouch like a kangaroo.

Crunch time

A seahorse has one skeleton inside
its body and one on the outside like
a suit of armor. This keeps it safe from
predators who don't like its crunchy body.

A seahorse wears a crown

Every seahorse has its own special crown called a "coronet." No two are the same, just like a human fingerprint.

Daddy cool

A male seahorse looks after the eggs in a pouch on his tummy.

A gripping tail

If a strong wave comes along, a seahorse grips a clump of seaweed with its long curly tail, to stop it being washed away.

JELLYFISH

Is a jellyfish made from jelly?

No! But a jellyfish has no bones so its body is soft and wobbly like jelly. A jellyfish actually isn't a fish at all.

Not half bad!
If a jellyfish is cut in half, it becomes two living jellyfish.

Jet-powered jelly

A jellyfish shoots water out of its body to push it through the water. If it gets tired, it drifts along on a current.

Glow-in-the-dark

Some jellyfish can glow in the dark. The light is off-putting to predators who don't enjoy a glowing dinner.

No-brainer

A jellyfish has no brain, blood, ears or heart.

OCTOPUSES

Why does an octopus need eight arms?

An octopus uses its arms in lots of clever ways.
Each arm has suckers and taste buds to help it pick
up and taste food. Its arms are full of brain cells,
so each arm has a mind of its own. Tentacool!

Ink-teresting

When an octopus is scared it squirts ink
into the water to confuse its attacker.
Some squid shoot glow-in-the-dark ink!

Fast movers

An octopus squirts a jet of water from the back of its head to push itself along. It can even use jet power to jump out of the water.

Can you find ...

... two squid that each have two extra-long tentacles as well as eight legs?

Did you know ...

... an octopus has three hearts?

WHALES

Why is a whale so big?

A whale can grow to be very big because the water around it supports its weight. The blue whale is longer than a basketball court and has a heart as big as a small horse. It is bigger than the biggest dinosaur!

Breath of fresh air

A whale breathes through a hole in its head. When a baby whale is born, its mum pushes it to the surface to take its first breath.

A humpback whale sends messages ...

... to its friends by slapping the surface of the water.

Wailing whales

Some male whales sing romantic low-pitched eerie songs in the hope that a lady whale will be listening.

Peas in a pod

A whale lives in a group called a pod.

CRUISING THROUGH A FAR-OFF OCEAN

CRABS

Why does a crab run sideways?

A crab's knees bend out to the side which means that it walks sideways. Our knees face to the front, so we walk forwards.

Oh snap!

A crab has two, big front claws. It uses them to cut up and crush its food and to pick things up.

A crab says "hello" by ...

... waving its claws. Crabs also send messages
to each other by tapping on rocks.

Good eye-dea

A crab has eyes on stalks just like
a snail. It can look for danger
in two directions at once.

A decorator crab ...

... covers itself with pieces of seaweed
and shells to hide from its enemies.

SEALS

Does a seal live in the sea or on land?

A seal spends most of its life in the sea but it has to come up to the surface to breathe air. A seal can sleep underwater or on the beach.

Wobbly walkers, nippy swimmers

A seal is slow at shuffling along the shore, but very quick and nimble when it's in the sea.

Breath taking

A seal can hold its breath underwater for up to 2 hours!

EXPERTLY NAVIGATING THE HIGH SEAS

Seal chase

A seal pup doesn't need to be taught how to swim. It loves to play chase underwater.

Watch out!

Not all seals are friendly. A leopard seal is very vicious and can sometimes hunt and eat other seals for dinner.

SHARKS

Do sharks eat people?

There are over 500 types of shark and they all eat meat. Sometimes sharks bite people by accident if they mistake them for a seal or big fish. Sharks don't hunt humans.

Did you know ...

... most fish have 4 pairs of gills but most sharks have 5?

Toothy tots

A baby shark loses a set of teeth inside its mother's tummy before it is even born.

Stomach-turning table manners

A tiger shark shoots its stomach out of its mouth to give it a rinse after a meal.

Just keep swimming

Some fast sharks have to swim with their mouths open to filter enough water to be able to breathe. If they slow down, they suffocate!

29

KRILL

What on earth is krill?

A krill looks a bit like a shrimp. There are more krill in the sea than any other animal on the planet! Lots of sea creatures depend on having plenty of krill to eat.

SWIRLING IN A PINKY-HAZE IN THE OCEAN

Inner beauty

A krill has a see-through body, which means you can see it digesting last night's dinner.

Far out, man!

Sometimes krill form big swarms that make the sea look pink. Krill swarms have been seen from space!

Twinkle, twinkle little krill

Some krill have glow-in-the-dark insides so at nighttime they shimmer under the surface of the sea.

In for the krill

A blue whale can eat up to 4 tonnes of krill in one day!

Cruel crustaceans

A krill usually eats plants but if it is very hungry, it might eat the krill next to it.

DRAGONETS

Does a dragonet breathe fire?

No! A dragonet gets its name from its brightly colored frilly fins that make it look like a Chinese paper dragon.

Slime alert!

Sometimes, a dragonet cloaks itself in a stinky slime to stop it from being eaten.

Walking on water

A dragonet swims along the bottom of the sea. Its fast-moving fins make it look as though it is walking on the sea floor.

Big yourself up

A male dragonet has a long spine
on his back that he sticks up
to make himself look bigger.

Fin-tastic moves

A male dragonet performs a special
frilly-fin-dance to attract a female.

Tiny dragon

A mandarin dragonet is only 6cm long.
Like all dragonets, it has thick skin instead
of scales to protect it from sharp rocks.

SEA SNAKES

How can a snake live underwater?

A sea snake is very good at swimming. It has a flat tail that is uses like an oar to help it swim quickly through the water. It has to come up for air but can hold its breath for a long time underwater.

A sea snake sheds its skin ...

... every 2-6 weeks to get rid of barnacles that grow on its body.

Can you find ...

... an eel? It has a long, ribbon-like fin along its whole body.

Salty spit

A sea snake filters out salt from its blood and spits it back into the sea.

Rings of danger

Sometimes a sea snake has colorful rings on its body that say "I'm poisonous!"

35

DEEP-SEA FISH

What do deep-sea fish have in common?

Deep-sea fish look very strange. They live in the cold, dark bottom of the sea and have to survive under the weight of tons of water pressing down on them from above. There is very little food or oxygen, so deep-sea fish have adapted in special ways.

Anglerfish

A female anglerfish has a light bulb hanging from her head. When other fish swim up to investigate, she snaps them up.

SKULKING IN THE INKY DARKNESS

36

Ogrefish

This fish has long, sharp fangs that point
inwards to stop its prey from escaping.
It looks scary but can only grow to 15cm long.

Gulper eel

The gulper eel has a big mouth
and stretchy stomach to catch
as much food as possible.

Blobfish

A blobfish has a squashy body
that is compressed into a blob
under the pressure from above.

SWORDFISH

Does a swordfish have a sword?

A swordfish's nose is sharp and pointy like a sword. It uses it to slash and stun its prey. It can even use it like a knife, to cut food into smaller bits.

Sun seeker

A swordfish loves to bask in shallow water and soak up the warm sunshine.

Toothless wonder

When a baby swordfish grows up, it loses all its teeth!

Sword aboard!

A swordfish can be strong and aggressive. It can even pierce the hull of a boat.

One fast fish

A swordfish can swim at up to 50 miles-per-hour. It is one of the top-ten fastest fish in the world!

RAYS

Does a ray make electricity?

There are many types of ray. Only electric rays make electricity in their bodies. They use their electricity to shock predators or prey, and to send messages.

Water wings

A ray has huge wing-like fins. When it flaps them, it looks as though it's flying underwater.

SOARING ABOVE THE OCEAN FLOOR

Ray wash while-u-wait

A manta ray often visits cleaning stations where other fish eat its dead skin.

Stingrays

A stingray has poisonous spines in the middle of its tail. It uses them to catch other fish for dinner.

Breathing back-up

A ray breathes through gills under its body. When it lies on the sand, they are covered up so it breathes through back-up holes on its head.

CORAL REEF FISH

Is a coral an animal or a plant?

A coral is a type of animal. When there are lots of them all together, they make an underwater forest called a reef. Plants grow here, too. Reefs are home to many types of special fish.

Parrotfish

A parrotfish uses its beak-like mouth to scrape tasty algae off stones and coral.

Clownfish

A clownfish lives inside a sea anemone. The anemone's stinging tentacles guard the clownfish when it is inside its home.

RAINBOW SCHOOLS DART THROUGH THE BUSY REEF

Surgeonfish

A surgeonfish has spines that are as sharp as knives on its tail. It uses them to spike its enemies.

Boxfish

A boxfish is square. Its bones are rigid like a suit of armor so it can't move quickly. Other fish find boxfish too hard to eat.

Lionfish

A lionfish has colorful stripes that say "I'm poisonous" to bigger fish that might try and eat it.

TUNA

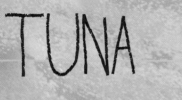

How many tins can one tuna fill?

A bluefin tuna can live for 40 years, grow up to 10 feet long and weigh more than a horse! It could fill more than 5,500 tins.

Torpedo tuna

A tuna has a super streamlined body which helps it to glide through the water.

Aaalll by myseeeelf!

A tuna has no home. It spends every day of its life swimming across different oceans.

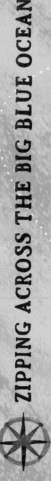

ZIPPING ACROSS THE BIG BLUE OCEAN

44

Plenty in the tank

A tuna is a strong and muscular fish.
It can swim very fast, for a long time,
and cover big distances.

What does a tuna have in its sandwich?

As a carnivore, a tuna also likes to eat fish for lunch.

PENGUINS

Why don't penguins freeze?

A penguin has a thick layer of fat all over its body that keeps it warm. A penguin parent-to-be stops its egg from freezing by balancing it on its feet.

Black and white and hard to spot

A penguin is camouflaged when swimming. It looks dark like the sea from above, and pale like the sky from below.

WHIZZING THROUGH ICY ANTARCTIC WATERS

What a grind!

A penguin swallows rocks and pebbles to help it grind up food inside its tummy.

Underwater acrobat

A penguin can't fly like other birds, but it "flies" along gracefully underwater.

Heavy bones

A penguin has heavy bones that help it dive underwater.

PUFFERFISH

What makes a pufferfish puff?

A pufferfish is slow so it can't get out of the way of predators very quickly. To put off hungry passers-by, it takes in lots of water and expands into a spiky ball.

A fish without scales

A pufferfish has thick stretchy skin instead of scales.

SLOWLY SWIMMING THROUGH A WARM CURRENT

Toothy can-openers

Beak-like teeth help a pufferfish to prise open mussel and clam shells.

In the blink of an eye

A pufferfish is the only fish that can blink. Its eyes can also move in two directions at once.

Most poisonous fish in the world!

The pufferfish is also the second most poisonous animal after the poison dart frog.

DOLPHINS

Why do dolphins jump out of the sea?

A dolphin is very clever and loves to play. It enjoys racing others and seeing who can make the biggest splash. A spinner dolphin can turn 7 times in the air!

Smell I never!

A dolphin breathes through a hole at the top of its head. It is like a nostril but a dolphin has no sense of smell.

JUMPING THROUGH THE CREST OF A WAVE

Can you spot ...

... something that doesn't belong in this habitat?

Hearing things

Instead of ears, a dolphin hears by feeling vibrations through its head and jaw bones.

Dolphin clicks

A dolphin talks to its friends by making clicking sounds underwater.

Half-asleep

A dolphin sleeps by resting one half of its brain at a time.

TIDE POOLS

What can you find on the beach?

When the tide goes out tide pools are left behind. They are a good place to look for creatures who like warm shallow water. Here are some of the top things you can spot at the beach.

Barnacle

A barnacle can come in all kinds of colors. It has a hard shell and sticks to rocks, boats and whales.

Butterfish

This fish is as slippery as butter! It is long, and wriggly and covered in spots.

Sea anemone

An anemone looks like a flower, but it is actually an animal. It is pretty but has a nasty sting!

Mussel

A mussel clings to rocks with its hairy beard. It opens underwater and closes in the air.

Starfish

A starfish isn't a fish at all! It can have up to 40 arms and has no blood.

Lemon sea slug

This sea slug is sour like a lemon to stop things from wanting to eat it.

HOW DEEP?

Where in the sea do creatures live?

Different animals have evolved to live at different depths in the sea. Some live at the top where it is light and easy to pop up for air. Others live at the bottom where it is dark and spooky.

Sunlit zone

Most sea creatures live here. This zone is close to the surface so it is bright and warm.

Twilight zone

Fish in this zone have large eyes to see in the low light. It is home to sperm whales, giant squid, lanternfish and viper eels.

450 ft

*Not to scale

—3,200 ft

Midnight zone

Sea cucumbers, vampire squid and frilled sharks live here. They have flabby bodies to cope under the weight of the water above them.

—13,000 ft

Abyss

The dumbo octopus lives here as well as lots of worms, and snails. It is cold and covered in sludge that falls down from above.

—20,000 ft

Hadal zone

Deep sea trenches make up the hadal zone. It is home to sea pigs, which are a type of cucumber.

OCEANS IN DANGER

Is the sea in trouble?

Most of the planet is covered in water but we are not always good at taking care of it. There are many things that humans do that can damage the sea and the creatures that live there.

Big ships

Large ships spill harmful oil into the oceans. Their noisy engines make it difficult for sea mammals to communicate.

Overfishing

Some types of fish are almost extinct because we have caught and eaten too many of them.

Global warming

Humans have burned lots of fossil fuels, warming up the planet. This means that sea levels have risen and sea water has become more acidic, making it hard for some sea life to survive.

PLASTIC IN THE SEA

How does our garbage pollute the sea?

Lots of plastic garbage ends up in the sea. This harms animals and their habitats. We can help to stop this by using fewer things made from plastic.

The break down

Unlike natural materials such as wood, plastic takes 400 years to break down.

Danger

Sea creatures can choke on plastic garbage. Sometimes large fish eat lumps of plastic which make them sick.

Chemicals

Plastics contain harmful chemicals which damage the seawater and the habitats of sea creatures.

DID YOU FIND...

... all the things from the "Can you find?" questions and the 15 hiding places of the special sardine from the beginning of the book?

20-21 Octopuses

12-13 Sea turtles

26-24 Seals

16-17 Seahorses

28-29 Sharks

18-19 Jellyfish

30-31 Krill

32-33 Dragonets

42-43 Coral reef fish

34-35 Sea snakes

46-47 Penguins

38-39 Swordfish

52-53 Pufferfish

40-41 Rays

54-55 Dolphins

FISHY PHRASES

How to talk like a sea life expert

Here are some words to use when talking about animals that live in the sea.

Where do sea creatures live?

A **marine animal** lives in **salt water**. A large area of salt water is called a **sea** and a big sea is called an **ocean**.

The place that a sea creature chooses to live is called its **habitat**. A **coral reef** is a habitat that is home to many types of sea creature.

Sea creatures can live on their own, but some types of fish live in a big group called a **school**.

60

When the sea moves down the beach at night, and moves back up during the day, this is called the **tide**. Under the sea, water moves in different directions and this is called the **current**.

All living things have their own place in the **food chain**. This is decided by what they eat and what eats them.

Lots of fish and whales eat **plankton**. Plankton is a microscopic creature that is the first link in the food chain.

INDEX

To my brilliant nephew,
Or Zommer with love

Thanks to my editor Lucy Brownridge and my designer Aaron Hayden

First published in 2018 in the United States of America by Thames & Hudson Inc., 500 Fifth Avenue, New York, New York 10110

www.thamesandhudsonusa.com

Reprinted 2018

Library of Congress Control Number 2017959972

ISBN 978-0-500-65119-3

Printed and bound in China by Reliance Printing (Shen Zhen) Co., Ltd.